A Guide to

ALASKA SEABIRDS

Written by Nancy E. Stromsem
Illustrated by Charlotte I. Adamson

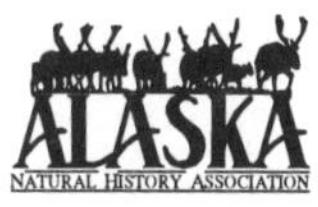

Published by the
Alaska Natural History Association
in cooperation with the
Fish and Wildlife Service,
U.S. Department of the Interior.

A Guide to Alaska Seabirds

Written by Nancy E. Stromsem.
Illustrated by Charlotte I. Adamson .
Special editorial assistance by Patrick J. Gould, Douglas J. Forsell and other staff of the U. S. Fish and Wildlife Service.
Much of this material is taken directly from Arthur L. Sowls, Scott A. Hatch and Calvin J. Lensink, *Catalog of Alaskan Seabird Colonies,* published in October 1978 by the U.S. Fish and Wildlife Service.
Project coordination by Catherine Rezabeck.
Book design by Clark Mishler & Associates.

Second edition 1989.
Project coordination by Frankie Barker.
Design additions by Lisa Dunham.
Illustrations pages 9, 17,18, & 19 by Lisa Dunham.

Third edition 1995.
Project coordination by Lisa Dunham.
Cover design by After Hours Design.
Printed by Northern Printing, Anchorage, Alaska.

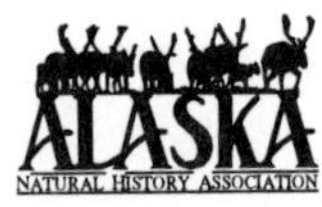

Published by the Alaska Natural History Association
in cooperation with the U.S. Fish and Wildlife Service,
U.S. Department of the Interior.

ISBN Number 0-9602876-4-7

Table of Contents

(continued next page)

Table of Contents

Gulls *(Continued from Page 3)*

Terns

Auks & Puffins

Map of Alaska

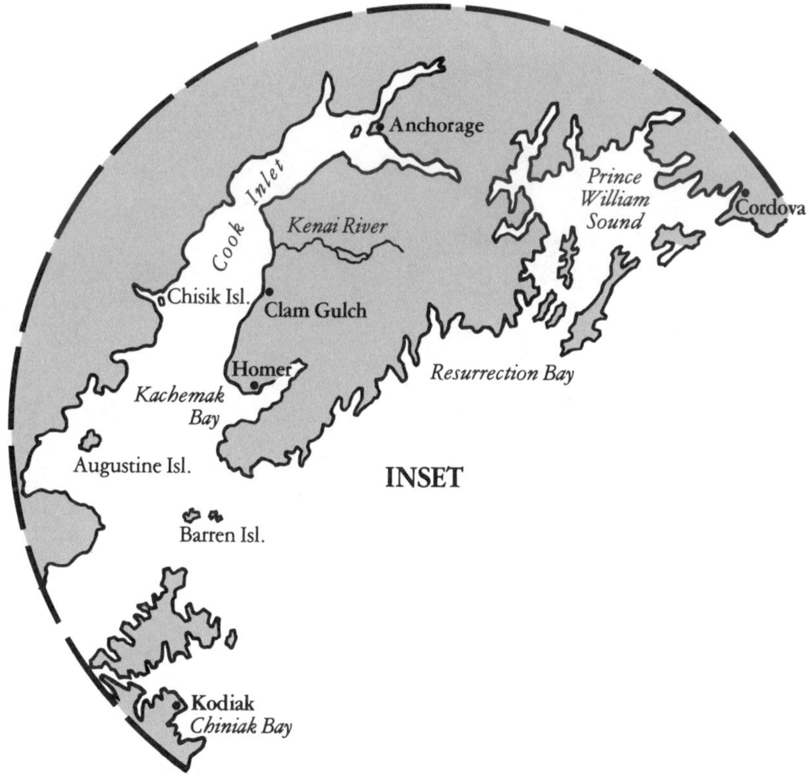

INSET

Nesting Sites of Seabirds

Flat Ground
Glaucous Gull
Glaucous-winged Gull
Arctic Tern
Aleutian Tern

Burrow
Fork-tailed Storm-Petrel
Leach's Storm-Petrel
Ancient Murrelet
Cassin's Auklet
Rhinoceros Auklet
Tufted Puffin

Cliff Ledge
Common Murre
Thick-billed Murre
Northern Fulmar

Cliff
Black-legged Kittiwake
Red-legged Kittiwake
Double-crested Cormorant
Pelagic Cormorant
Red-faced Cormorant

Rock Crevice
Horned Puffin

Talus
Fork-tailed Storm-Petrel
Leach's Storm-Petrel
Ancient Murrelet
Cassin's Auklet
Parakeet Auklet
Crested Auklet
Least Auklet
Whiskered Auklet

Boulder Rubble
Pigeon Guillemot
Black Guillemot

Introduction

Brightly colored puffins, smoothly soaring albatrosses, raucous colonies of gulls—the coastal and marine resources of Alaska have a wonderful vitality. By the millions, seabirds feed from Alaska's bountiful waters. In summer their numbers may equal or exceed the number of seabirds in the remainder of the northern hemisphere. This book is designed to help Alaskans and visitors to Alaska enjoy one of our most delightful, as well as plentiful, resources.

The book was inspired by a more detailed volume, the *Catalog of Alaskan Seabird Colonies*, published in October 1978 by the U.S. Fish and Wildlife Service. Many of the illustrations, maps and some of the text of this book are taken directly from it; however, this is not just a pared-down version of that book. Tips about identification and details about behavior have been added to assist observers in recognizing the birds.

Readers should realize that not all of Alaska's seabirds are covered here. An extraordinary diversity of marine birds breeds in Alaska, and many others visit from distant seas. Over 73 species have been identified in the Gulf of Alaska alone, and barely half of them are included here. Alaska's common breeding seabirds are described, as well as some of the most common summer visitors.

The species are presented in taxonomic order. This is the scientific classification of plants and animals according to their natural relationships. Identification aids include descriptive text, illustrations and range maps. The birds are pictured and described in their adult, summer (breeding) plumage.

The text begins with suggestions about where to find the species, followed by a section on identification. In cases where the bird may be confused with another species, there is information about how to distinguish one from the other. A third section deals with behavior, specifically, any tendencies to travel in flocks, pairs, or alone; recognizable flight characteristics; and feeding habits. The final paragraph tells about nesting. A few species inspired deviations from that outline!

Range maps illustrate where in Alaska to look for various species. These maps will also generally reflect breeding localities since most species presented here breed in Alaska during the summer.

A more detailed state map locates places mentioned in the text and may help readers not thoroughly familiar with Alaskan geography. For those who wish to record their sightings, the table of contents is designed to double as a check list. One last item to note is the illustration on the opposite page, "Nesting Sites of Seabirds," a guide to the species that nest in various types of coastal habitat.

When identifying a seabird it is important to take note of the clues given in the pictures and text. These clues are general size and shape, color (especially note where dark and light patches are located), special behavior, and habitats. Some birds may appear not to fit any of the pictures; seabirds can vary in color according to age or the season, so look at more individuals if possible. And sometimes birds just don't stay around long enough for you to get a good look—keep watching, and good luck!

Albatross

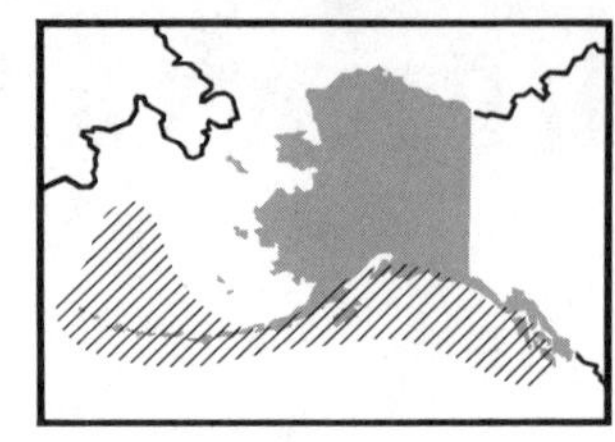

Albatrosses visit Alaskan waters during the summer. They usually stay far out at sea. If you have the opportunity to take an ocean-going vessel out beyond the continental shelf, you may see one. With luck, it may follow your ship. They are known for wandering great distances, often following ships. Laysan albatrosses are more common than black-footed albatrosses in western Alaskan waters and the southern Bering Sea, whereas black-footed albatrosses are more common than Laysans in eastern Alaskan waters. Short-tailed albatrosses, once the most numerous albatross in the Aleutians, are now on the endangered species list. After heavy exploitation by plumage hunters on their Japanese island breeding grounds, they were thought to be extinct in the 1940s but were later found breeding in small numbers. Their range, as well as their population, is expanding now; but the likelihood of sighting one is nearly nil.

Laysan albatrosses are predominantly white with dark brown or black on the upper wings, back and tail. The underside of the wings is light with dark patterns around the edges. This albatross has flesh-colored legs and a bill that varies from yellow with a grayish tip to mostly gray. If you think you spot one, be sure to notice the back color, since that's the key feature that distinguishes the Laysan albatross from its endangered relative, the short-tailed albatross.

Black-footed albatrosses are dark-bodied birds. Upper parts are dark brown or black and under parts are gray-brown. They have dark bills and, of course, black feet. Some individuals have large areas of white around the bill and rump.

Short-tailed albatrosses look like Laysan albatrosses except the short-tailed albatrosses have a white back.

Long, narrow wings and effortless, gliding flight characterize albatrosses. Their wing spans reach over seven feet, and they have been seen planing close to the water's surface for as long as seven minutes without flapping their wings. They eat fish, squid and offal.

Albatrosses are noted for longevity; life expectancy is about 36 years.

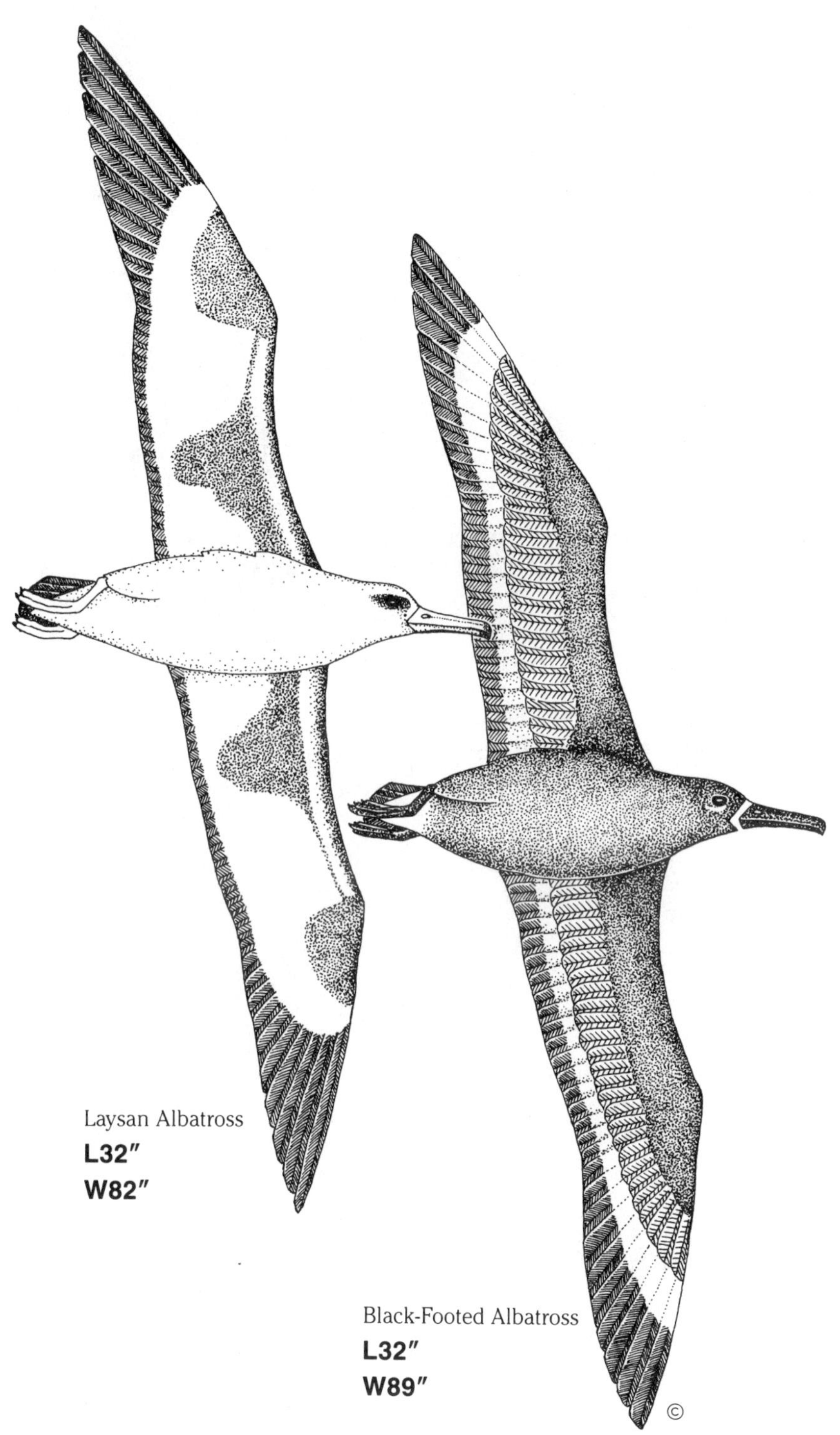

Laysan Albatross
L32″
W82″

Black-Footed Albatross
L32″
W89″

©

Northern Fulmar

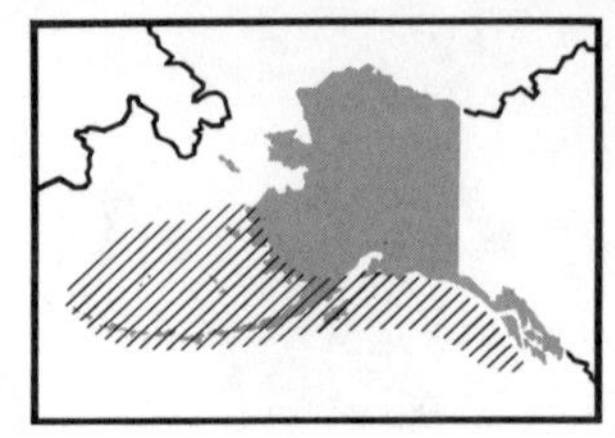

You may spot a northern fulmar anywhere in Alaskan marine waters at any time of the year; however, they are particularly abundant over deep waters beyond the continental shelf. So, the general rule is, the farther out you go, the more likely you are to see one.

The color of northern fulmars ranges from a dark bluish-gray to predominantly white. At colonies in the Bering Sea, light-phase birds predominate. At more southerly colonies, dark-phase birds predominate. One fairly consistent field mark is a lighter patch of feathers, triangular in shape, located beyond the bend in the wing. Look for the short, thick, yellow to yellow-gray bill to avoid confusing fulmars with sooty and short-tailed shearwaters. Also, fulmars are chunkier than shearwaters.

In flight fulmars hold their wings stiffly, alternating fairly rapid wing beats with long glides. They normally disperse widely at sea, but they follow ships, and huge flocks may gather around fish-processing vessels to scavenge on offal. They also flock around reefs or the edges of currents where food—small fish, squid and crustaceans—churn to the surface. They may forage hundreds of miles from their breeding colonies.

Fulmars nest on islands and cliffs, usually in association with other cliff nesters such as murres and kittiwakes. The fulmars frequently choose the upper, vegetated portions of the cliffs. They have a low reproductive rate, but a long lifespan—sometimes more than 50 years.

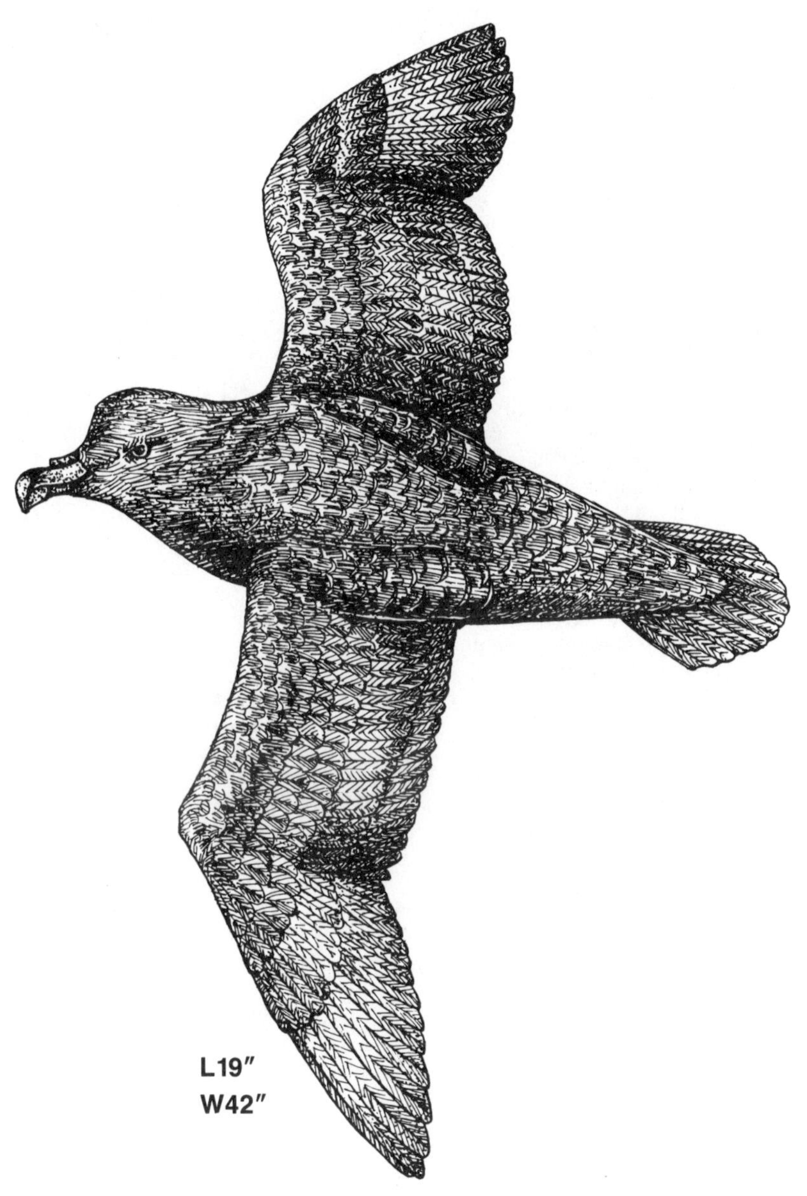
L19″
W42″

Shearwaters

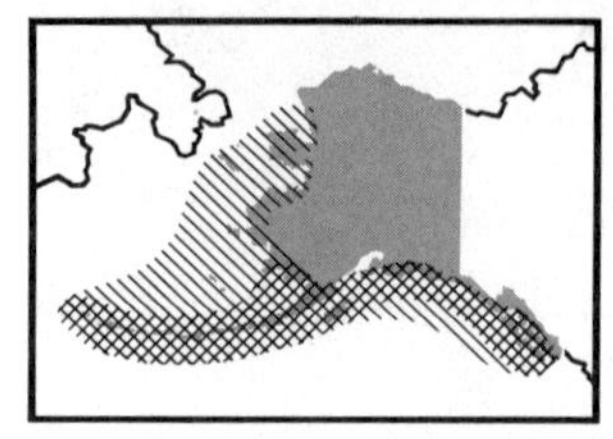

If you're riding the ferry in summer, stay alert, and you'll surely see a shearwater or, more likely, a large flock of them. Short-tailed shearwaters are the most abundant birds in Alaska in the summer; sooty shearwaters rank second. Flocks of many thousands of shearwaters are not uncommon, and occasionally assemblages of over a million are sighted in the Bering Sea. Sooty shearwaters are the predominant species in the eastern Gulf of Alaska, whereas short-tailed shearwaters are far more abundant than sooty shearwaters in the western Gulf and the Bering Sea. The Barren Islands are a hot spot for shearwaters. Bird watchers also have great success in Kodiak Harbor, at the mouth of Cook Inlet around Augustine Island, and at the mouth of Kachemak Bay.

Differentiating sooty from short-tailed shearwaters in the field is difficult. Both have dark brown plumage except on the underside of the wings. They both have slender, black bills. Although coloration under the wing is variable and may be dark to light in either bird, the underwing markings provide the most reliable means of differentiating the two species.

The **sooty shearwater** has a large, irregular white patch that covers most of the underside of the wing. As it flies overhead, its wings appear a mixed pattern of light and dark.

The **short-tailed shearwater** has a silvery sheen on all feathers under the wings. The silver reflects light consistently, making the entire underwing appear bright white in the sun or gray on cloudy days.

If you think you're watching shearwaters, try to get a good look at the slender bill as that's a good key to distinguish sooty and short-tailed shearwaters from more thick-billed fulmars and uncommon pale-footed shearwaters.

Both sooty and short-tailed shearwaters are sometimes referred to as "whale birds" by fishermen, due to their habit of congregating around whales, apparently to feed on krill, fish and squid brought to the surface by the mini-currents created by the whale's swimming.

Sooty Shearwater
L19″
W43″
Short-Tailed Shearwater
L14″
W38″
©

Fork-Tailed Storm-Petrel

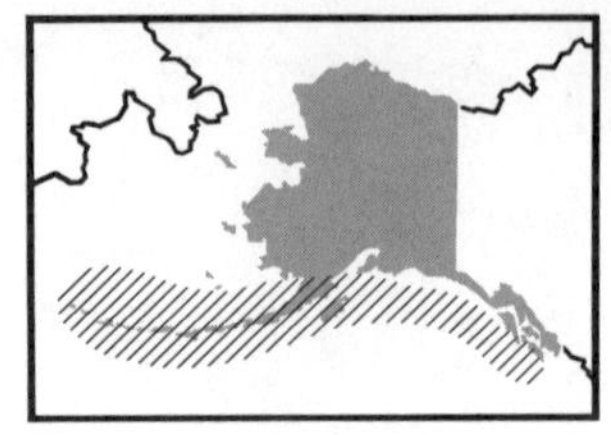

If you're out in a fishing boat with lights, this bird is the one most likely to drop in on you. In summer it's fairly common in marine waters all around the southern half of the state. You're not likely to see one near shore; but, when the weather's exceptionally stormy at sea, they sometimes seek refuge in calm bays. Generally, the farther out you go, the more likely you are to see a fork-tailed storm-petrel.

Among the smallest of Alaskan seabirds, fork-tailed storm-petrels are pearl gray above, blending to whitish below. Light and dark colors contrast on the underside of the wings, as depicted. The bill and legs are black. Of course, the tail is forked.

The flight of storm-petrels is swift, darting and erratic. They normally feed at the surface on small crustaceans and other plankton, and are also attracted to offal spilled from fishing vessels and to drifting carcasses of whales and seals. The Eskimos called these birds "oil eaters" as they appeared to skim the oily surface of water around wounded whales and seals.

Storm-petrels are nocturnal on land, so their colonies are difficult to locate. It appears, though, that they nest wherever a comfortable hole presents itself. They may nest in talus or other natural cavities, dig their own burrows, or nest in unoccupied burrows of other birds.

Leach's Storm-Petrel

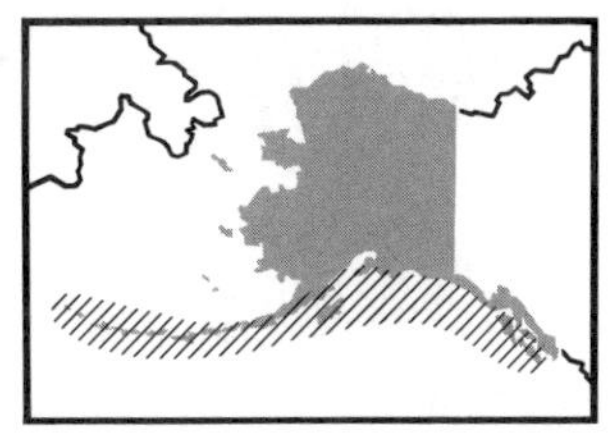

To see a Leach's storm-petrel, you'll have to go way out to sea or visit their breeding colonies. You're far less likely to see a Leach's than a fork-tailed storm-petrel.

Leach's storm-petrel is sooty blackish-brown all over except for a white rump patch. It has a black bill and legs. In lighting conditions where it's difficult to recognize color shades, the white rump patch is the easiest way to tell Leach's from the more common fork-tailed storm-petrel.

These birds tend to fly an irregular course, with sudden, swift changes in direction. They forage in areas where waters are 2,000 meters deep, or deeper, on a variety of zooplankton which they obtain at the water's surface. They forage over vast areas, even during the nesting season.

Parents share responsibility for incubating the egg, alternating care in shifts of several days. Since the returning adult comes to the nest late at night, their breeding grounds are hard to locate. Although they seem to prefer to dig their own burrows, these storm-petrels sometimes nest in unoccupied burrows of tufted puffins.

L8″

Cormorants

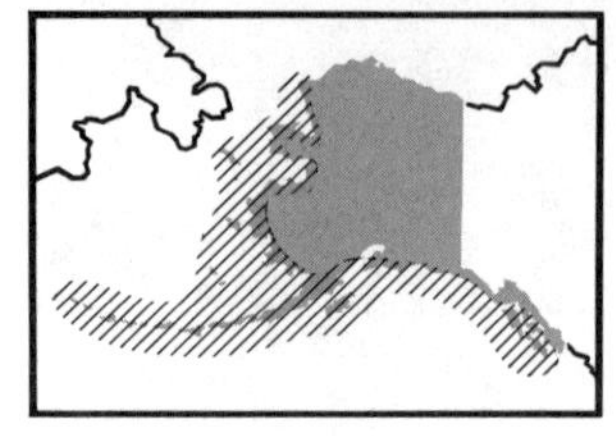

Four species of cormorants occur in Alaska. In order of most to least abundant they are red-faced, pelagic, double-crested, and Brandt's cormorants. Common to all these cormorants are certain characteristics that make them easy to recognize, including bold upright posture, shiny black plumage, feathers that absorb water, consequent posing with wings spread to dry, hooked bills and snake-like necks, which are sometimes the only part above water as they swim.

Brandt's cormorants, at the northernmost extremity of their range, are sometimes sighted in southeast Alaska and as far north as Prince William Sound. They are large cormorants with blue throats.

Double-crested cormorants inhabit both fresh and saltwater areas on the coasts of the Gulf of Alaska and Bristol Bay. They have yellow throats.

Pelagic cormorants may be found anywhere along the Alaskan coast where there are cliffs for nesting and rocks for roosting. They are smaller than other cormorants. They have some deep red color on the face, but it's a smaller area than on the red-faced cormorant and can't be seen from a distance.

Red-faced cormorants have bright red faces. The red extends back beyond the eyes. Listen up bird listers! These cormorants are found only in Alaska and possibly the Commander Islands of the USSR. There's a good chance of seeing them along the ferry routes in the Gulf of Alaska anywhere near shore between Cordova and Kodiak. In the past, red-faced cormorants have been seen nesting on Gull Island, an easy tour from Homer.

Cormorants tend to travel in small flocks, often flying along the shore in lines or "V" formations. Double-crested cormorants fly with their necks crooked and their heads up; Brandt's cormorants fly with their necks slightly crooked or straight out; the others fly with their necks straight out. Cormorants rarely stray more than a few miles from shore. In inshore waters they capture a variety of fish and bottom-dwelling crustaceans by diving and underwater pursuit. Their feathers absorb water, enabling them to lose buoyance and improving their ability to dive and swim underwater.

It's rare for a Brandt's cormorant to occur this far north and, if any breed here, there are probably less than a hundred. The other three species share mixed colonies as their ranges overlap. Cormorants do not necessarily return to nest in the same place year after year. For colony sites they usually choose precipitous cliffs, although the double-crested cormorant may choose more gradual slopes, flat islets, or even trees for nest sites.

Pelagic Cormorant
L26″
W39″

Pomarine Jaeger

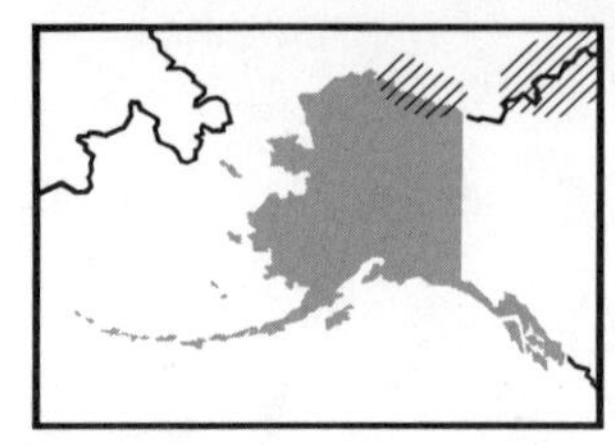

The largest, most rotund jaeger, the Pomarine Jaeger has regular, purposeful wingbeats noticeably slower than those of the Parasitic Jaeger. Its bill is also larger and the adult's tail streamers form flat, twisted knobs at the tip. Its black wing linings are visible at a distance. A white patch near the wing tips is visible at closer range. Most of the adult Pomarines are light beneath with some barring but there are instances of nearly all black coloring. Juveniles are usually strongly barred on back and underneath and tail streamers are nearly invisible. In all ages, the white at the base of the primary feathers is more extensive than in other jaegers.

The Pomarine Jaeger breeds on low, wet tundra interspersed with lakes and ponds. It is known to chase large gulls and will migrate along marine waters inshore and off. It winters at sea.

L21″
W48″

Parasitic Jaeger

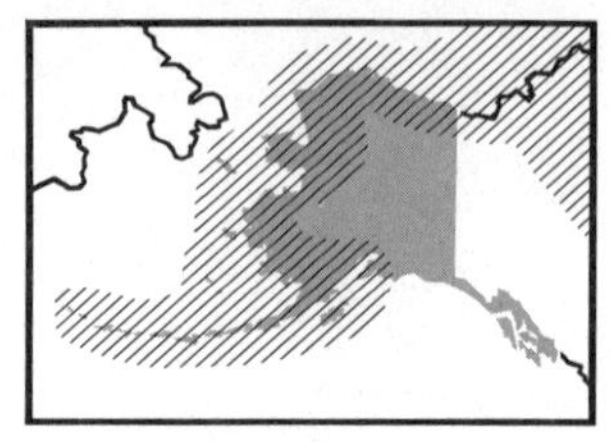

Jaegers are predatory seabirds with long, central tail feathers and pointed, angled wings. The adult plumage may take up to four years to develop, and variable plumages during growth phases make identification a challenge.

The Parasitic Jaeger is of medium build, neither bulky nor slight, and has a swift wing stroke. In all phases there is a light touch of white on the upper wings and pointed tail streamers. The light-phase juvenile has muted barring below as compared to the pronounced barring of the dark-phase juvenile. Both juveniles have a distinctive rufous-brown tint and gradually lose their barring with age.

The Parasitic Jaeger breeds on low tundra and in stony areas. It is rarely seen inland, preferring the Alaskan shores and the Aleutian Chain. Of the three types of jaegers (Pomarine, Parasitic and Long-tailed), the Parasitic and Long-tailed can be commonly seen in Alaska, the Parasitic most frequently.

L19″
W42″

Long-tailed Jaeger

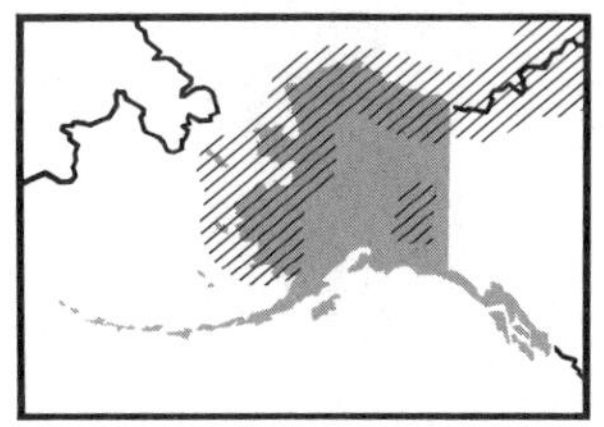

The Long-tailed Jaeger is the most graceful jaeger, due to its ternlike flight and long, pointed tail streamers. Its light build is offset proportionately by these tail streamers in all ages, although the juveniles are more rounded.

In all plumages, there is a noticeable contrast between the gray-beige mantle or back and the darker flight feathers. An adult jaeger lacks the white patch on the underwings and the strong barring evident on the juveniles, as well as the grayish overall tone. Some juveniles also exhibit a very light head and nape.

The Long-tailed Jaeger migrates along marine waters, sometimes far offshore. They nest on the wet coastal tundra and dry up-land tundra of the Interior.

Glaucous Gull

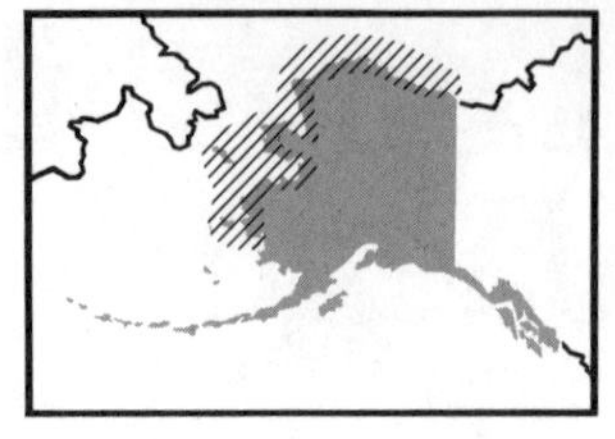

Glaucous gulls frequent coastlines, bays and harbors from Nunivak Island northward along the coasts of the Bering Sea and the Arctic Ocean. On very rare occasion, one strays into the Gulf of Alaska during the summer.

Glaucous gulls are the largest gulls in Alaska. They're mostly white with a pale gray back. Legs are flesh-colored or yellowish. The bill is yellow with a bright red spot on the lower mandible. If you think you've spotted one, check the wing tips. Wing tips should not have any black or gray. If the wing tips are white, it's either a glaucous gull or an uncommon ivory gull. Ivory gulls are smaller than glaucous gulls, and they have black legs. Glaucous gulls also resemble glaucous-winged gulls. Glaucous gulls are the larger, paler, and normally the farther north of those two species.

Glaucous gulls are on the wing a lot. They fly gracefully, with slow, continuous wing beats. Noted as predators, they steal food from birds of other species and, throughout the breeding season, raid nests of other birds for eggs and young.

They nest in scattered pairs or small groups, closely associated with other species. Nests of grass, seaweed, moss and debris are placed on slightly elevated ground or, more often, on cliffs or ledges.

Glaucous-Winged Gull

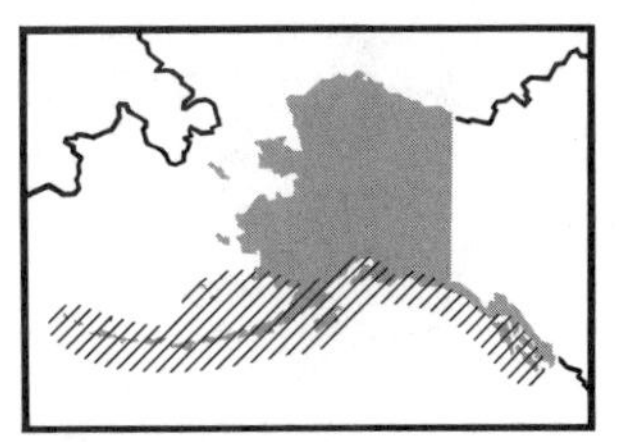

Ubiquitous is the word to describe these gulls. They are abundant, and they inhabit all types of water from fresh to deep offshore. Lured to the artificial food supplies associated with human settlement, they are common in the maritime provinces of Alaska. Groups of 10 to 500 may be seen loafing on rocks or beaches. You may spot them anywhere around the Gulf of Alaska or the southern Bering Sea, but near Kodiak is probably the best place to look.

Glaucous-winged gulls are large, white birds with gray backs. Their wing tips are gray with just a spot of white at the rear edge of the feathers. Their legs are pink. Like herring gulls and glaucous gulls, these have a yellow bill with a red spot on the lower mandible. Many of the gulls you'd see loafing during the breeding season are nonbreeding birds less than four years old. Because they still retain some of their immature color pattern, they look dirty.

Glaucous-winged gulls often travel in groups, which may be quite large as they leave an area en masse after feeding. They are omnivorous and highly opportunistic in their food habits. Far at sea they eat a variety of pelagic fish and crustaceans. In tidal zones they eat crabs, limpets and sea urchins. Garbage and offal draw them to harbors and, in season, they'll go up salmon streams to feast on spent salmon. They also eat insects and small mammals. Around their colonies they prey on eggs, young and adults of their own as well as other species.

At large, multispecies colonies, it's typical for the glaucous-winged gulls to make up only a few tenths of a percent of the total population. They nest on sandbar islands, the tops of more rugged islands, along beaches and also on cliffs. Nests are usually grass-lined scrapes.

L26″
W58″

Herring Gull

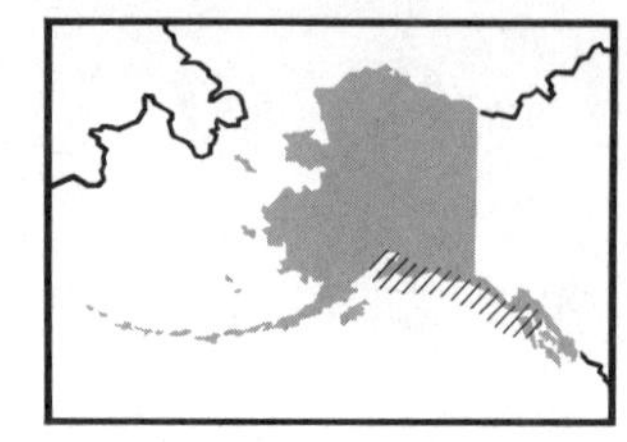

In Alaska herring gulls are principally freshwater birds, but can be found in coastal areas, lagoons, estuaries and at the heads of large bay systems. If you're bird watching around Glacier Bay, Kachemak Bay or along the waterfront in Anchorage, there's a chance you'll see one. Like glaucous-winged gulls, they are often found loafing in groups along beaches and on rocks. They seldom venture far from land in summer but, beginning in October, some move offshore and they may be found hundreds of miles from shore through early spring.

These are large gulls, predominantly white with pearl gray backs. Their wings have black tips with white spots just along the rear edge. The wing tips are the key to distinguish herring gulls from glaucous-winged gulls. Herring gulls also resemble Alaska's other inland gull, the mew gull, so check the overall size, the bill for shape and color, and the legs for color. Herring gulls are larger than mew gulls, have longer bills, which are yellow with a red spot on the lower mandible, and have pinkish flesh-colored legs.

Their graceful flight, with slow but strong wing beats, resembles that of the glaucous-winged gull; and the two species often travel in mixed flocks. Herring gulls gather in noisy numbers at garbage dumps and canneries to feast on waste; but they also forage for carrion, live fish, and a variety of inter-tidal prey. Inland, their diet may include insects, small mammals and berries as well as fresh-water fishes and invertebrates. Also, other species of seabirds—adults, eggs, and young—fall prey to herring gulls.

Their colonies are located on the margins of inland lakes and streams as well as on sea strands and islands. Generally nests are simple depressions on the ground, sparsely lined with grass, moss, seaweed, or other plant material.

Mew Gull

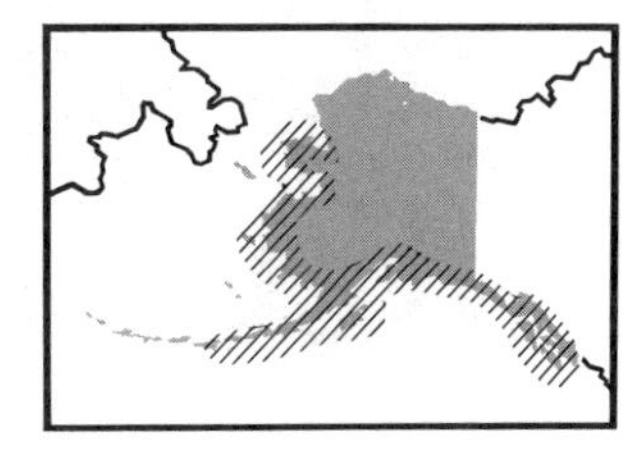

These are the gulls most people see at Denali National Park in the summer or in freshwater or coastal marshes around Anchorage. In winter they are particularly abundant in inside waters of southeast Alaska. Both summer and winter they tend to remain near shore rather than heading out to sea.

These small gulls are predominantly white with pearl gray backs and white-spotted, black wing tips. Their plumage is the same as the herring gulls.' Mew gulls differ from them by being smaller, having yellowish legs and very short, unmarked greenish-yellow bills that earned them their other name, short-billed gulls. Mew gulls also resemble black-legged kittiwakes. Their general body and head shapes are alike. To differentiate, notice the white on the wing tips of mew gulls and their yellow, not black, legs.

A large flock of fairly small gulls is likely to be kittiwakes. Mew gulls tend to be more solitary than other gulls and are much less vocal than kittiwakes. Along the coast mew gulls eat small, surface-shoaling fish. They forage on beaches and mud flats for a wide variety of intertidal marine life and are also attracted to garbage dumps, canneries, and salmon spawning streams.

Interior nesting mew gulls scatter along streams, lakes and marshy tundra, rarely forming distinct colonies. Coastal populations may form small colonies on mainland beaches, sandspits, and on islands of low relief. Nests are usually placed on the ground, but occasionally in trees.

L16"
W43"

Black-Legged Kittiwake

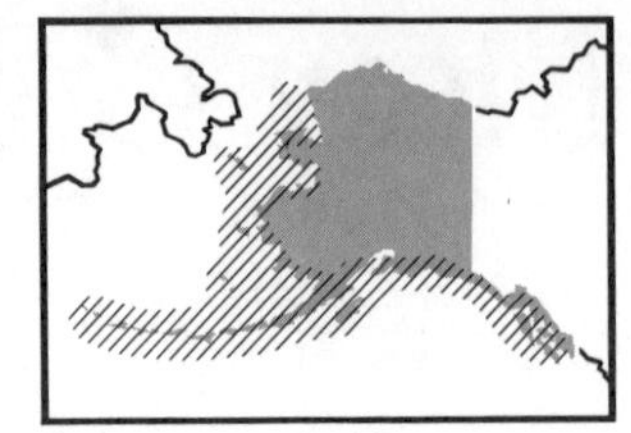

This is a familiar species almost everywhere on the Alaskan coast. Black-legged kittiwakes are found in just about every type of water from deep offshore to estuaries and lagoons. They often bathe in fresh water as well. Look for them whenever you're at the beach—clamming at Clam Gulch, ambling along the Homer Spit, or fishing in Resurrection Bay. You will also see them from the ferry in Prince William Sound. If all else fails, a tour from Homer to Gull Island will surely produce.

Black-legged kittiwakes are small gulls, predominantly white with gray backs. The wing tips are solid black both top and bottom. They have yellow, spotless bills and, of course, black legs. They are similar in size to mew gulls.

Observers have characterized kittiwake flight as a rowing motion, with shallow wing beats and a lighter, more buoyant flight than most gulls. They are often found in large flocks, especially if they are feeding. Even during the breeding season, they range far from land. Their food, consisting primarily of small fish and crustaceans or other invertebrates, is obtained at or near the water's surface.

Kittiwake colonies are noisy and conspicuous. Sites include offshore islands, rocks, and mainland cliffs. Although most colonies are located next to the open sea, some are found in fjords. Nests of grass, moss, or other plant materials and mud are typically constructed on precipitous cliff faces.

Red-Legged Kittiwake

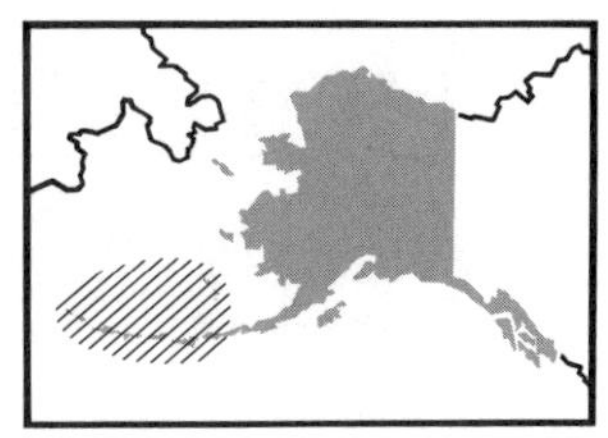

For the birder who has everything, we recommend a trip to the Pribilofs to tick the red-legged kittiwake off a bird list. Ninety-seven percent of the world's red-legged kittiwakes nest there on St. George Island. For the birder who hasn't got a trip to the Pribilofs, there's some consolation. Red-legged kittiwakes are highly pelagic; that is, they range far out at sea. Although records are few, there have been sightings in the Gulf of Alaska.

Except for obvious red legs and a few subtle differences, red-legged kittiwakes look like black-legged kittiwakes. They are predominantly white with gray backs and black-tipped wings—that's both top and bottom. For the experienced birder, the subtle differences are a shorter bill, rounder head, and darker wing linings than their black-legged congeners.

If you're willing to use "rowing" to describe the flight of black-legged kittiwakes, use it for the red-legged as well. Red-legged kittiwakes prefer to forage offshore and regularly go beyond the continental shelf. They feed primarily on small fish by plunging from some height above the surface.

Red-legged kittiwakes share all their known breeding grounds with black-legged kittiwakes. On St. George Island, the red-legged kittiwakes tend to nest higher up on cliffs, but at other sites they have been seen nesting side by side. Nests are similar to those of black-legged kittiwakes, except they're somewhat smaller and built more often under overhangs.

Red-Legged Kittiwake
L15″
W33″

Bonaparte's Gull

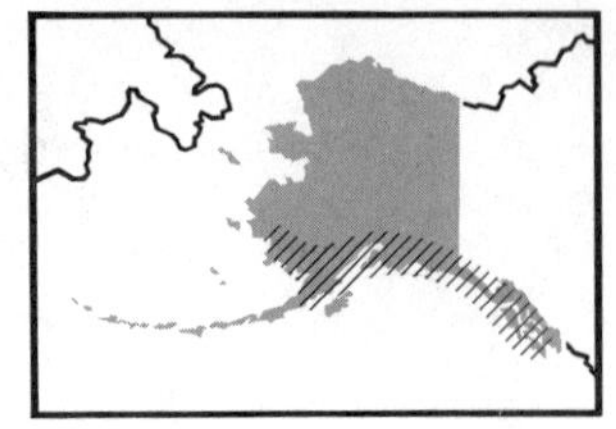

Fishing for salmon on the Kenai River will likely produce a Bonaparte's gull for your list. During summer they are found most commonly along streams and rivers throughout inland areas of central and western Alaska. Outside of breeding season they frequent coastal areas and become particularly common near glaciers and along waterways of southeastern Alaska during fall migration.

This small gull has a black head and white wedges on the fore edge of the wings. The bill is black, and the legs are bright red.

Buoyant, graceful flight is evident, especially during feeding. They eat insects while inland. In coastal areas, they also eat small fish and crustaceans. After leaving breeding areas, these gulls often travel and feed in loose flocks.

They build nests of small sticks and twigs lined with moss in conifers of wooded muskeg areas.

Sabine's Gull

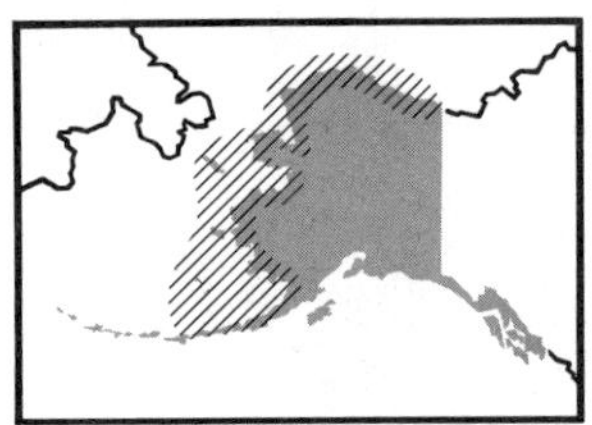

Sabine's gulls breed along the Arctic and Bering Sea coasts from Demarcation Point to northern Bristol Bay. You could see them during summer along coastal areas of the Yukon-Kuskokwim Delta, or perhaps along the road from Nome to Teller.

In Alaska, Sabine's is the only gull with a forked tail and one of only two common gulls with a dark head. Distinctive features include a slate gray head, gray back, flashy white triangles on the rear edge of the wings, and black wing tips. The remaining plumage of this small gull is white. Look for black legs and yellow on the tip of the black bill.

Sabine's gulls have light, buoyant flight and usually travel alone. They feed largely on insects caught in the air or picked up from the surface of ponds. They sometimes forage on mud flats and along margins of sloughs. Along the sea coast they may drop lightly to the water, and just as their feet touch, snatch small crustaceans or fish and fly on.

They nest in grass-lined depressions in low, wet tundra, either in small colonies or as scattered pairs.

Bonaparte's Gull
L13½"
W33"
Sabine's Gull
L13½"
W33"

Arctic Tern

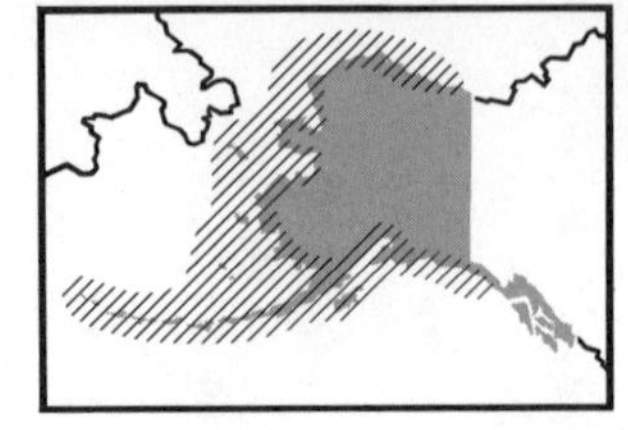

Arctic terns are common in coastal areas of the Gulf of Alaska and the eastern Bering Sea. They frequent coastal lagoons. An easy place to see them is on the road just south of Anchorage. They breed at Potter's Marsh.

Arctic terns are small, graceful birds. They are predominantly white with black on the top of the head and back of the neck, gray on the back, and silver-gray at the tips of their long, pointed wings. They have forked tails. Beaks, legs and feet are deep red.

They are gregarious, noisy and protective. That is, they attack people who approach too close to their nests. Their graceful flight is like a barn swallow's with rapid wing beats and frequent hovering and darting. While looking for fish they patrol the water with their beaks pointed down, and that is one way to distinguish them from small gulls, which fly with their beaks held horizontally. They prefer a diet of small, smelt-like fish.

Arctic terns breed throughout the interior region as well as along the coast. They nest near fresh or salt water on sandspits, beaches, rocky shores and islands, or on wet tundra. The nest is a small depression on the ground, lined sparsely with grass, or not at all. They nest in small- to medium-sized colonies or as scattered, isolated pairs. Nest sites are frequently moved from year to year in response to predators and other factors; only the largest colonies tend to persist at the same locations.

The Arctic tern has the longest migration known. It is the only seabird breeding in Alaska that travels as far as the Antarctic to winter. Travelling 11,000 miles each way, twice a year, it stays in daylight at polar regions more than any other species.

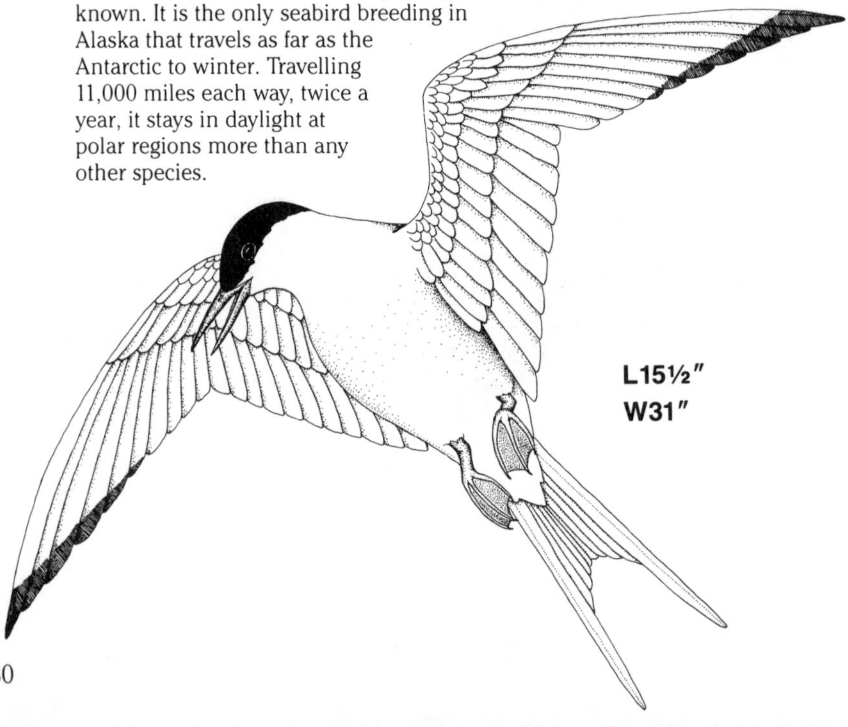

L15½"
W31"

Aleutian Tern

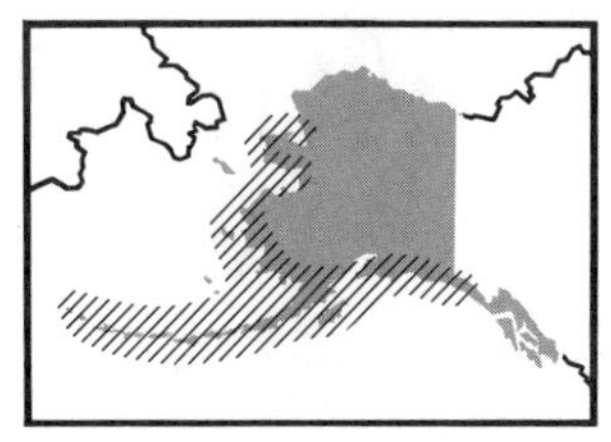

In some of the same coastal areas frequented by Arctic terns, you may spy a second, less common species, the Aleutian tern. Homer is one of the more convenient places to see them.

Resembling the Arctic tern, the Aleutian tern is slightly smaller, somewhat darker and has black bill and legs. Another distinctive feature is the white forehead, as pictured. Observers should be aware, though, that Arctic terns in winter plumage—as late as May and as early as August—also have white on the forehead, but there's a definite difference. The Aleutian tern has a sharply outlined white streak, more like a racing stripe, whereas the Arctic tern's white patch is larger and less well defined, more like a balding head. Their very different calls are also a good key to differentiation. The Aleutian tern uses a three note whistle, whereas the Arctic tern has a harsh cry.

Like Arctic terns, Aleutians have a very graceful flight, but their wing beats are slightly slower than the Arctic tern's. They forage a little farther offshore than Arctic terns. For their own dining pleasure, they choose krill; but they feed small fish to their young, perhaps to minimize the number of trips necessary between foraging areas and the nest.

All known colonies of Aleutian terns are located on or very near the coast. They frequently occur with Arctic terns in mixed colonies. Their nesting habitat includes sandspits, sandbar islands, or the flat, vegetated tops of rugged islands. The colonies may shift location from year to year.

L13½″
W29″

Murres

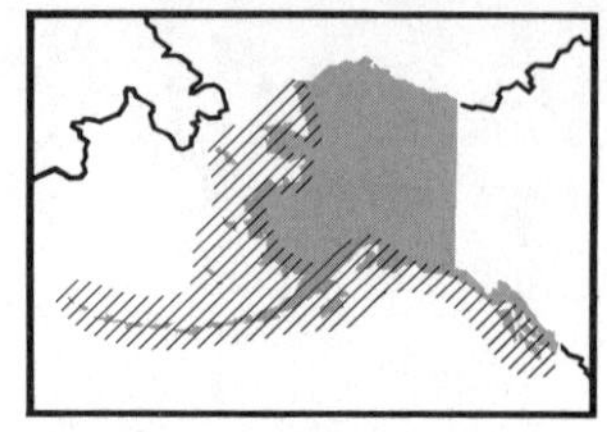

Common and thick-billed murres are found throughout Alaskan marine waters. Common murres make up a higher proportion of populations in the Gulf of Alaska, whereas thick-billed murres tend to outnumber common murres in the Bering Sea. Collectively, murres are probably the most numerous of all pelagic birds breeding in Alaska, and you're almost sure to see one if you're in a boat in the western Gulf of Alaska.

Murres are sufficiently different from other seabirds as to make them readily recognizable; however, it takes a discriminating bird watcher (and a bird watcher lucky enough to get close) to tell the difference between a common and a thick-billed murre.

Common murres have a more brownish head and back, a thinner bill, and less of a point where the bird's white breast joins the black neck.

Thick-billed murres have a blacker head and back, a thicker bill, which sometimes, but not always, has a white stripe at the edge, and a sharp point near the throat where the white breast meets the black neck.

Murres are highly gregarious. They fly and rest on the water in large flocks, particularly large in winter. They dive for food, and Alaskan fishermen have reported catching murres in crab pots set as deep as 65 fathoms, or 390 feet! Murres prey on small, herring-sized fish and larger marine crustaceans; the particular species in the diet vary both seasonally and locally.

During breeding season murres congregate on cliffs and ledges. Colonial nesting is highly developed, and a shoulder-to-shoulder arrangement on the nesting ledges is the rule. Murres are notable for the complete absence of any nest-building behavior. They lay their single egg on bare ground or rock ledges.

Thick-Billed Murre
L18″

Black Guillemot

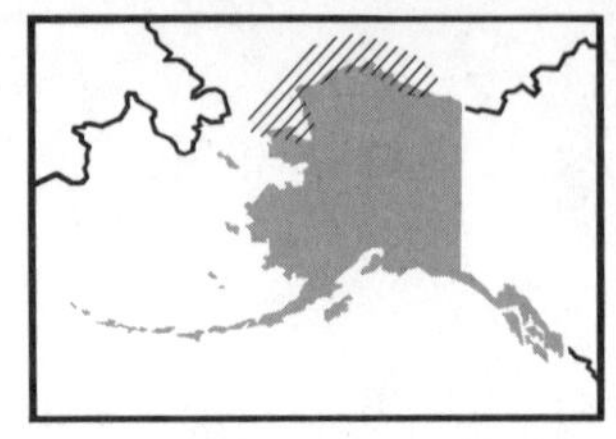

This bird is very similar to the pigeon guillemot, but it only nests in the far north. However, if you happen to be collecting driftwood along the barrier islands of the Beaufort Sea or on the Chukchi Sea coast, you'll have a good chance of running across one of Alaska's more uncommon marine bird residents. Black guillemots stay in inshore waters or leads in the ice along the northern coast.

Their plumage is all black except for some white on and under the wings. Large, all-white wing patches distinguish them from the very similar and more common pigeon guillemot, which has black wedges intruding into the white of its wing patches. Black guillemots also have striking red coloring on the legs and inside the mouth.

They are usually seen in low numbers, and their flight is characteristically rapid and close to the water. They are good swimmers; they dive to forage on or near the bottom for small fish, crustaceans and marine worms.

Black guillemots nest either in loose colonies or as solitary pairs. Natural cavities in talus, on boulder beaches, or on rock cliffs provide suitable nest sites. On the Chukchi and Beaufort Sea coasts, guillemots nest on barrier islands composed of sand or gravel and largely devoid of vegetation and local relief. They inhabit piles of driftwood and various types of man-made debris, and their nesting range is probably limited by the presence or absence of such features. Their range may be expanding along with development of the Arctic.

L13″

Pigeon Guillemot

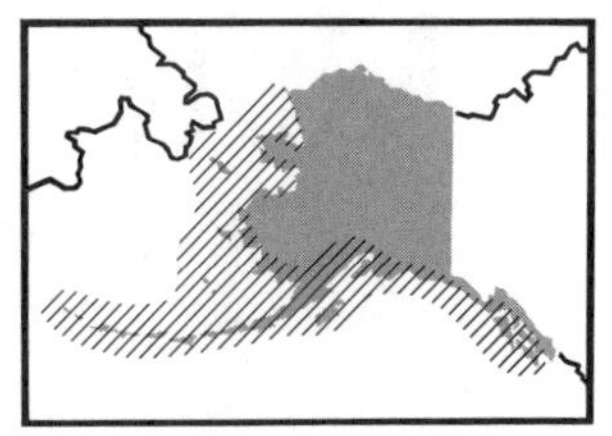

This species is common along the entire coastline of Alaska, but its frequency decreases as you get farther south or farther offshore. Look for pigeon guillemots along rocky shores, or take a tour from the Homer Spit out to their Gull Island nesting grounds. Listen while you watch. Their sustained, high-pitched whistle is distinctive and can be heard at quite a distance.

Like the black guillemot, it's all black except for white on the wings and red on the legs and inside the mouth. Pigeon guillemots have smaller white areas on the wings than do black guillemots, and a couple black crescents or wedges intrude into the white patches. If you don't get a good look, chances are you've seen a pigeon guillemot, unless you're on the Arctic coast. They are far more common than black guillemots.

You tend to see pigeon guillemots not in flocks, but rather one here, two there. They fly rapidly, close to the water, and they rarely stray more than a few miles from land. They dive for small fish, usually just outside the surf.

Where large numbers of guillemots occur, they usually form colonies. In many areas, however, breeding pairs are distributed ubiquitously, at low density, along rocky coastlines. They typically nest in natural cavities in boulder beaches, talus slopes, and broken cliffs at low elevations. They may also nest in unoccupied burrows of tufted puffins or, occasionally, dig their own burrows.

Murrelets
(Marbled and Kittlitz's)

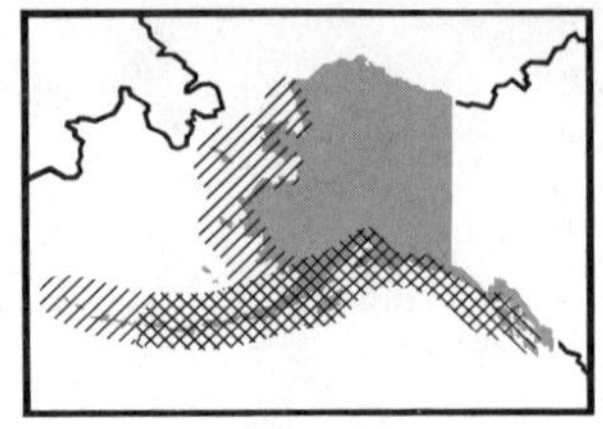

These closely related birds share the distinction of being the least known of Alaskan seabirds, at least with respect to their activities on land. They are common in bays and fjords and are most abundant in inshore waters from southeastern Alaska to Kodiak Island. Kittlitz's murrelets are also common along the Alaskan Peninsula and throughout the Aleutians. Marbled and Kittlitz's murrelets are some of the most abundant birds in Prince William Sound.

Both species have dark brown backs, white patches where wings meet back, and white bellies, which you don't see when they're on the water. The white patches distinguish them from all other similar birds except least auklets. Even for experts, the distinction between Marbled and Kittlitz's murrelets requires close inspection.

Marbled murrelets are darker brown and darker all the way to the water line. The soft notes whistled between marbled murrelet pairs are distinctive and help in identification.

Kittlitz's murrelets have more golden backs and get lighter towards the water line. Their call is more of a deep squawk than a whistle.

Deep, fast wing beats and a rocking motion characterize murrelet flight. They tend to travel in pairs. Murrelets dive to feed primarily on small fish and crustaceans. Although they generally forage close to shore, the distance between feeding grounds and inland nest sites may be considerable.

Very few nests of either species have been found. Apparently neither species is colonial, and they visit land only at night. Marbled murrelet nests have been found as far as 20 miles inland, and Kittlitz's, 35 miles. Marbled murrelets have a unique nesting behavior for a seabird; they nest on the limbs of large old evergreen trees, except that in southwestern Alaska they also nest on the ground. Kittlitz's murrelets apparently nest in rocky, alpine habitat up to several thousand feet in elevation, as well as on steep sea slopes.

Marbled Murrelet

Kittlitz's Murrelet

Ancient Murrelets

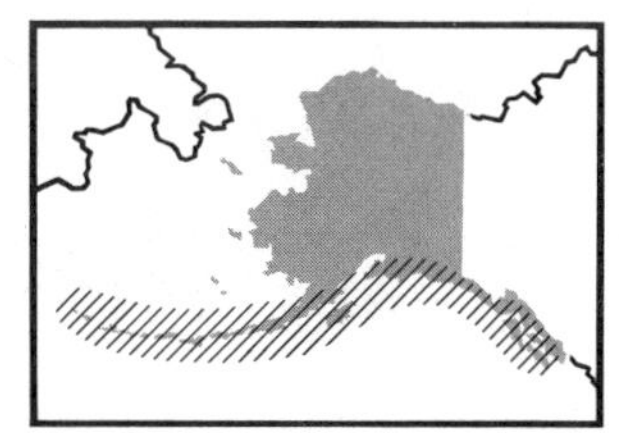

Ancient murrelets can be anywhere in the Gulf of Alaska, Bristol Bay or the Aleutians. They tend to spend their time offshore, over the continental shelf; however, they are sometimes seen from the ferry in Prince William Sound, in Resurrection Bay, or Kachemak Bay.

They have black caps and throats, gray backs, white underparts, a yellow bill, and a white stripe over the eye.

Except during the short breeding season, ancient murrelets generally live offshore. They travel in small bands, diving for small crustaceans and fish.

Ancient murrelets are nocturnal on their breeding grounds. They are colonial and nest in burrows up to about a yard long, or in natural cavities under rocks, tree roots, or overhanging clumps of sod.

They are exceptionally precocious. About two days after the chicks hatch, the adult birds call to them from the sea. Under cover of darkness, the downy chicks make their way alone to the adult birds waiting in the water. They complete their development at sea under the care of the adults.

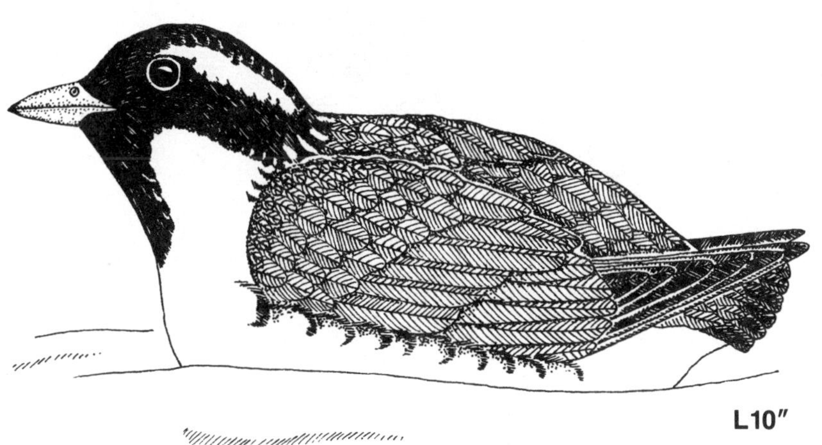

L10″

Cassin's Auklet

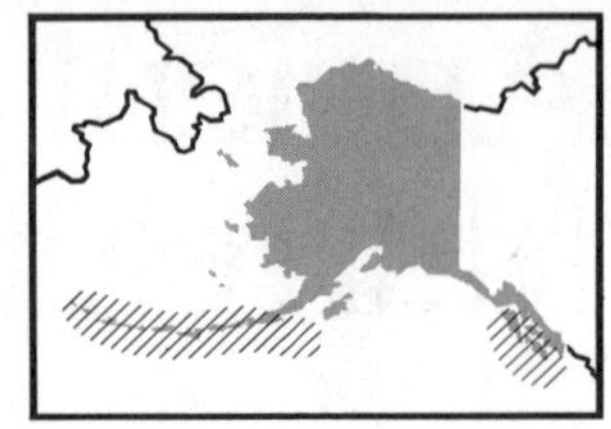

Cassin's auklets are abundant in southeast Alaska, and you're likely to see them from the ferry. They're found in shallow offshore waters of the Gulf of Alaska but tend to stay in eastern or western rather then central portions of the Gulf.

Cassin's auklets are little chubby birds that are dark above the water line and white below. Their dark bills are marked by a small white spot on the lower mandible.

They look quite round when they're in flight. They fly in a straight path, rapidly beating their short, stubby wings. The wings are a compromise in design that offers dubious efficiency above water, but also aids under water. They dive for planktonic crustaceans or other invertebrates, using their wings for propulsion.

Cassin's auklets are strictly nocturnal on their breeding grounds. Their nest sites are burrows. In southeastern Alaska they dig burrows under Sitka spruce or a heavy understory of salmonberry and grasses. Farther west, they occupy grassy slopes or areas of bare ground. Nesting densities are typically high, and in places this may lead to an absence of vegetation and consequent soil erosion.

L9″

Parakeet Auklet

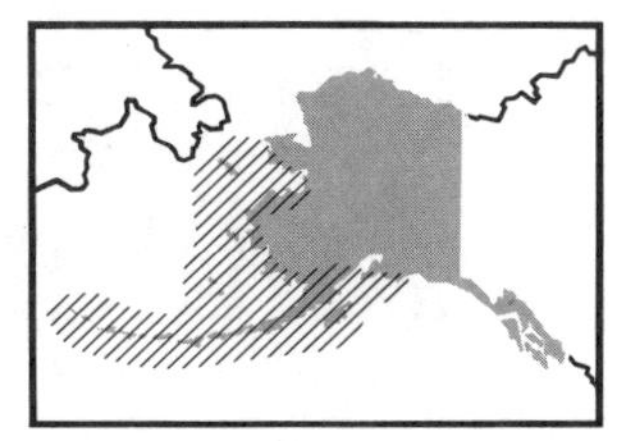

Although their center of abundance is the Bering Sea, parakeet auklets also breed on Chisik Island in Cook Inlet, around Prince William Sound and in the Barren Islands. They're more likely to be in shallow offshore waters than along the coast or in bays.

Parakeet auklets are plump birds. They have red, upturned bills, brown or gray heads and backs, white bellies, and single white plumes behind the eyes. They could be mistaken for rhinoceros auklets, but they're smaller than the rhinos.

Their flight pattern is usually rather direct, low over the water, and unfortunately, away. They scatter to feed on small crustaceans, which they obtain by diving. Like other auklets, murrelets and the puffins, they use their wings for propulsion underwater. After they finish feeding for the day, they group together on the water for a while before returning to the colonies.

Where their ranges overlap, parakeet auklets occur in mixed colonies with crested, least and whiskered auklets; however, the colonial tendency appears less strong in this species than in other auklets, and they often nest in small scattered groups or as solitary pairs. Parakeets nest deep within the rubble of talus slopes and in cracks and crevices on rocky shorelines or cliffs. Most of their nests are inaccessible to human observers as well as natural predators.

Crested Auklet

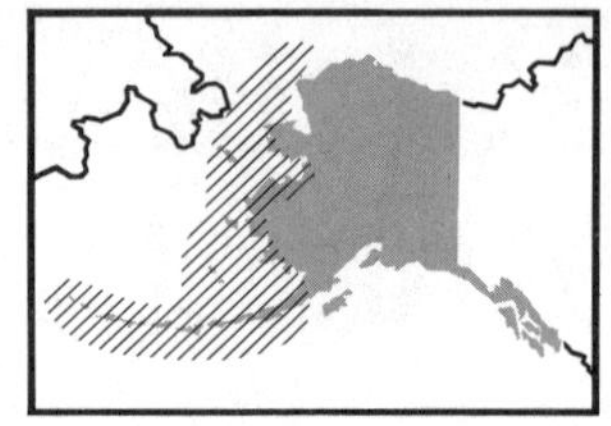

In summer crested auklets flock to the Bering Sea, and Aleutian and Shumagin Islands. Sometimes lesser numbers get as far east as Kodiak. In wintertime these birds are numerous in the bays around Kodiak.

They are slate gray, with bright orange bills and white plumes behind the eyes. Their crests are distinctive. Crested auklets also have a distinct odor. They smell like citrus fruit.

Flocking behavior is highly developed in crested auklets. Aerial displays by thousands of birds in dense, cloudlike flocks are unforgettable. In the summer of 1976 near Kodiak, a swarm of crested auklets, attracted to the night lights of a fishing boat, nearly sank the boat as crew members shovelled them off the decks. Like other auklets, they dive for small, planktonic crustaceans.

They frequently occur in mixed colonies with large numbers of least auklets and lesser numbers of parakeet auklets and whiskered auklets. Crested auklets nest in crevices in talus slopes, lava flows or cliffs.

Illustration by Anthony R. DeGange

Least Auklet

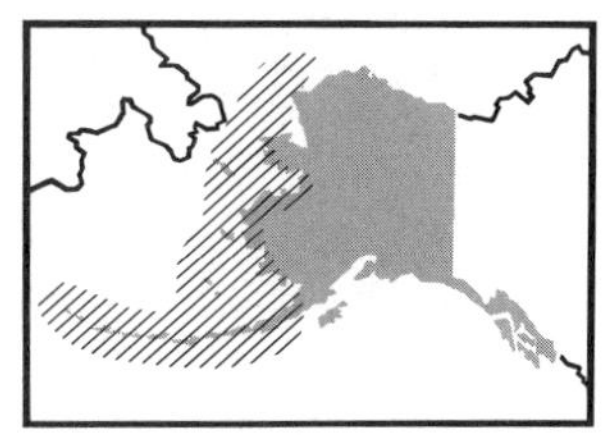

Least auklets are among the most abundant seabirds in Alaska, but their remote range makes them inaccessible to most bird watchers. In summer they stay close to their breeding colonies, which are mostly islands in the Bering Sea and the Aleutians. During migration, however, least auklets are sometimes sighted in the western Gulf of Alaska and even in Cook Inlet and Prince William Sound.

Least auklets, suiting their name, are the tiniest auklets. They are black on the upper parts except for white patches on the scapulars and white streaks on the forehead and face. The chin is black. The remaining under parts are white mottled with dusky.

Least auklets usually cluster in small groups of five or ten birds. Their flight, with rapid wingbeats in erratic patterns, has been likened to that of bumblebees. It's hard to get a look at them as they flush well ahead of ships. They feed, by diving, on planktonic crustaceans, primarily in nearshore water.

Least auklets commonly nest in enormous colonies in close association with other auklets. The largest colonies contain from 250,000 to a million birds, and the numbers of least auklets greatly exceed the others in most mixed colonies. Least auklets lay single eggs in bare rock crevices deep in talus or in small cavities in lava flows overgrown with vegetation.

Illustration by Arthur Sowls

L6¼″

Whiskered Auklet

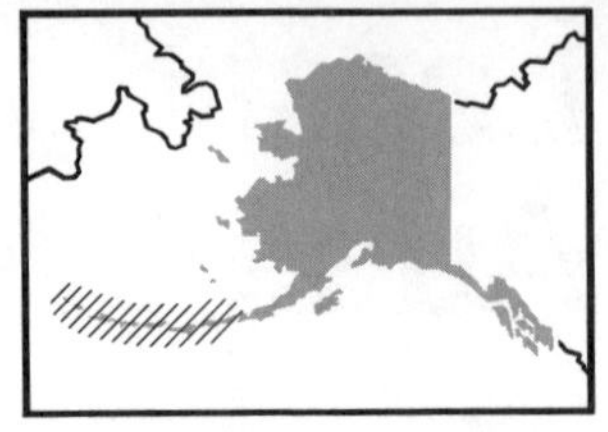

The worldwide distribution of whiskered auklets is very limited. There are only a few islands in the Aleutians where you might find them. A highly motivated bird watcher might fly to Dutch Harbor, obtain a boat and head into Avatanak Strait. Around Basalt Rock, in early afternoon, the prized whiskered auklet is likely to appear . . . and he's likely to appear surprised.

Whiskered auklets are small birds with slate gray backs, white underparts and bright orange bills. They have carried head plumes to the extreme. Each bird has seven: a black plume protruding from the forehead and three white plumes on each side of the face. In flight a whiskered auklet may be mistaken for a least auklet, but only one has head plumes.

They travel in small flocks. They change directions suddenly, land suddenly, scatter suddenly, and dive suddenly. Little study of their feeding habits has been carried out. Other auklets in their range eat planktonic crustaceans, and whiskered auklets probably have similar food habits.

They commonly nest in talus, in company with least and crested auklets. The apparent decline or disappearance of whiskered auklets from the most westerly islands of the Aleutian chain casts doubt on their status farther west; but, at least historically, they breed in the Kurile and Commander Islands as well as throughout the Aleutians. The largest known colony today is on Buldir Island.

L7¾"

Rhinoceros Auklet

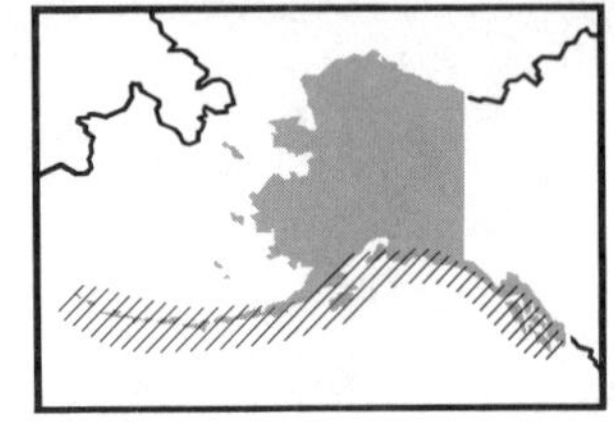

Rhinoceros auklets breed in small numbers throughout the Gulf of Alaska. They are most commonly seen in the Gulf's deeper waters, but occasionally a bird or pair will visit the outer portions of some of the bays. For instance, they have been sighted in Resurrection and Chiniak Bays.

They appear all dark when sitting on the water but show their white bellies in the air. Unusual head adornment includes not only white plumes but also a small yellow horn at the base of the yellow bill. They look a lot like a thin-billed version of a puffin.

With wings that are almost too small for their bodies, their flight is labored; takeoffs comical. Remember, the wings also function underwater! Rhinoceros auklets feed on small fish and crustaceans, using their wings to swim to considerable depths. After feeding they gather offshore for a while before turning in for the night.

They excavate burrows on grassy slopes or beneath forest canopies. Birds enter and leave colonies only at night, making detection of their colonies difficult.

L15″

Horned Puffin

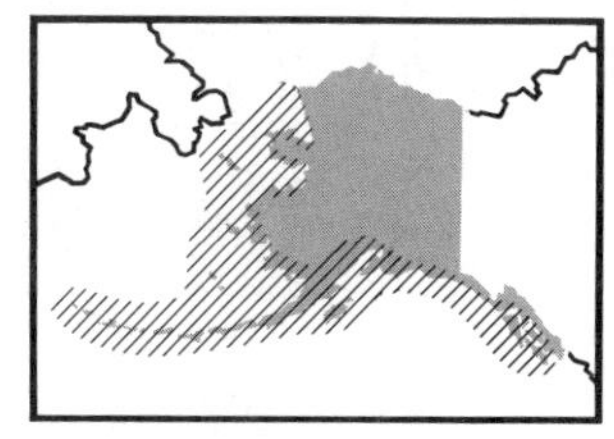

Horned puffins are found in bays or just off rocky headlands, riding swells in groups of two to ten. Their center of abundance in Alaska is off the southern coast of the Alaska Peninsula, somewhat west of Kodiak; however, they breed around Kodiak Island in large numbers, along Prince William Sound, in the Chriswell Islands near Seward and in lesser numbers in Cook Inlet. Boat tours out of Seward are one of the most convenient ways to visit puffin colonies.

Horned puffins have huge bright yellow bills with red on the tip. They have a small dark horn made of skin above each eye. Underparts are white except for a black collar. Feet are bright orange.

Puffins possess heavy wing loads. They flap vigorously to go short distances, but are capable of flying a long distance. They use wing propulsion to dive, mostly for small fish but also for cephalopods and crustaceans.

Horned puffins generally nest under beach boulders, in talus, or in crevices of cliffs.

Illustration by Arthur Sowls.

L15″

Tufted Puffin

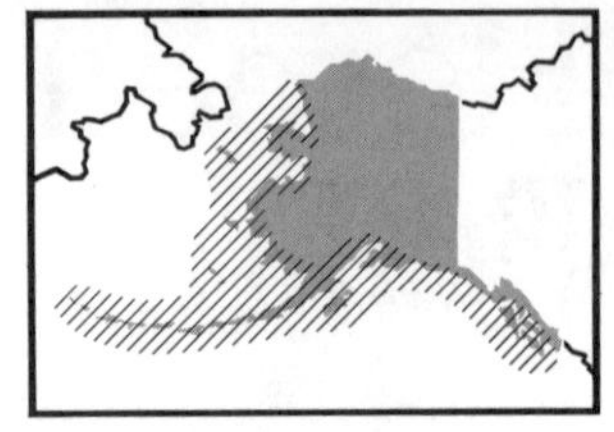

Of all seabirds in Alaska, this is the one most likely to be seen. Tufted puffins are abundant and can be in marine waters anywhere: near shore, offshore, in bays.

They have bright orange bill plates and orange-red feet. Their faces are white. The tufts are yellow. The rest is black.

They fly by flapping vigorously. Their diet is composed of small fish, cephalopods and crustaceans captured by diving. The wings are used for propulsion underwater. The large bill accommodates them in the chase. Small projections and grooves on the roof of the mouth and tongue help retain the first caught fish while the puffin continues to chase others.

Tufted puffins nests in burrows or, rarely, in rock crevices. Burrows often reach two meters in length and may have two or more entrances. In a typical colony, these puffins burrow on steep slopes or in soil along the tops of cliffs. Because tufted and horned puffins differ in their nest preference, the two species avoid competition for nest sites, allowing almost complete overlap in breeding distributions of the two species.

L15″

Field Notes

Field Notes